5—12

	DATE DUE	
	~~JUN 2 9 2012~~	
~~JUL 1 4 2013~~		

The Urbana Free Library

To renew: call 217-367-4057
or go to *"urbanafreelibrary.org"*
and select "Renew/Request Items"

MEDIKIDZ EXPLAIN DEPRESSION

rosen publishing's
rosen
central®

New York

Dr. Kim Chilman-Blair and Shawn deLoache
Medical content reviewed for accuracy by Dr. Mike Shooter

4|12
29 2

This edition published in 2011 by:

The Rosen Publishing Group, Inc.
29 East 21st Street
New York, NY 10010

Additional end matter copyright © 2011 by The Rosen Publishing Group, Inc.

Library of Congress Cataloging-in-Publication Data

Chilman-Blair, Kim.
Medikidz explain depression / Kim Chilman-Blair and Shawn deLoache.
     p. cm. — (Superheroes on a medical mission)
"Medical content reviewed for accuracy by Dr. Mike Shooter."
Includes bibliographical references and index.
ISBN 978-1-4358-9455-6 (library binding) — ISBN 978-1-4488-1837-2 (pbk.)
— ISBN 978-1-4488-1838-9 (6-pack)
1. Depression in children—Comic books, strips, etc. 2. Depression, Mental—
Comic books, strips, etc. I. Deloache, Shawn II. Title.
RJ506.D4C473 2011
618.92'8527—dc22

                            2010008833

Manufactured in China

CPSIA Compliance Information: Batch #MS0102YA: For further information, contact Rosen Publishing, New York, New York, at 1-800-237-9932.

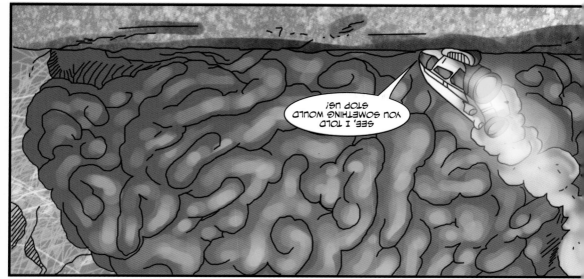

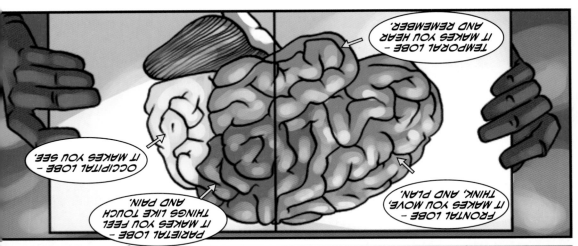

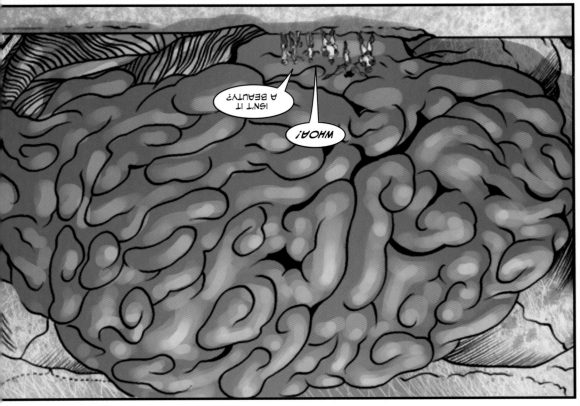